MW01259401

# The Miniature Horse

# The Miniature Horse

By Gail LaBonte

DILLON PRESS, INC.
Minneapolis, Minnesota 55415

## Acknowledgments

I owe many thanks to Barbara Norman of Winners' Circle Ranch in Petaluma, California, and to Pamela Gooby, who welcomed me to her ranch, Goose Downs, in Livermore, California. Rayford Ely of Oakland, California, and Daniel Barba, who manages the Ely miniatures, were very helpful. I also appreciate the help and information provided by Barbara Ashby of the American Miniature Horse Association, Robin Stallings of Ashly Acres, and to the people at the Land of Little Horses in Gettysburg, Pennsylvania. A special thanks goes to Elaine Matthews of Flying M Ranch in Ocala, Florida, for reviewing the manuscript.

The photographs are reproduced through the courtesy of Ashly Acres Miniature Horses; British Coal; Robert Dickinson; Gail LaBonte; Thomas Nebia; David Phillips; James and Vickie Shea; and Winners' Circle Ranch.

**Library of Congress Cataloging-in-Publication Data**

LaBonte, Gail.
  The miniature horse / by Gail LaBonte.
     p.    cm. — (A Dillon remarkable animals book)
  Includes bibliographical references.
  Summary: Describes the appearance, behavior, and rearing of the miniature horse and discusses its development, uses, and growing popularity in North America.
  ISBN 0-87518-424-3 : $12.95
  1. Miniature horses—Juvenile literature. [1. Miniature horses.  2. Horses.]  I. Title.  II. Series.
SF293.M56L33  1990
636.1—dc 20                       89-26046
                                         CIP
                                         AC

Dillon Press, Inc., 242 Portland Avenue South
Minneapolis, Minnesota 55415

Printed in the United States of America
1 2 3 4 5 6 7 8 9 10 99 98 97 96 95 94 93 92 91 90

# Contents

# Facts about Miniature Horses

**Scientific Name:** *Equus caballus*, the same name as other breeds of domesticated horses and ponies

**Range:** Owned and bred by people in Europe, North and South America, parts of Asia and Australia; becoming more widespread as numbers and popularity increase

**Description:**

*Height*—34 inches (87 centimeters) or less in height at the withers when fully grown

*Weight*—100 to 300 pounds (45 to 136 kilograms)

*Physical Features*—Should have the same proportions as a full-size or standard horse, but may have a longer and thicker mane and tail and thicker hooves for its size

*Color*—White, brown, or black in the same shades and combinations as full-size horses

**Distinctive Habits:** A curious and intelligent animal with all the same behaviors as full-size horses, but considered to be gentler, more affectionate, and more easily trained

**Food:** Wild grasses, hays, grains, vitamin and mineral supplements

**Reproductive Cycle:** Mares are ready to become mothers at 3 years of age; foal is born 11-1/2 months after mating and weighs between 18 and 22 pounds (8 and 10 kilograms); miniatures sometimes have difficulty with giving birth and need help from humans

**Life Span:** Usually 20 to 30 years, but some have been reported to live nearly 40 years

**Uses:** Are pets and companions for people of all ages and abilities; perform in shows and parades; pull people in carts and wagons

Miniature horses and a foal with their trainer at Flying M Ranch in Ocala, Florida.

# Chapter 1

# A Small, Small World

Imagine that you are in a corral full of horses. They whinny and snort, stamp the dirt with their feet, kick up their hooves, and chase each other at a gallop. Standing in the middle of these horses might be frightening. But you have no reason to be afraid because the horses are not much larger than big dogs!

Galloping across a pasture with manes and tails flying, these spirited animals look like creatures from a fairy tale. Some people can't believe their eyes when they first see them. Driving past a herd of little horses, passersby often turn around and come back for a second look.

Many people have not yet seen a miniature horse. When some of these horses were to be flown from Maryland to Washington, special wooden crates were delivered to the airport first. The workers loading the plane laughed and said, "You can't put horses in those little boxes!" They were surprised and delighted when the miniatures arrived in a van—the horses fit easily inside their carrying crates. In fact, many airlines now allow owners to fly these small animals in boxes as extra baggage.

Unlike powerful larger horses, which must be handled with care, miniature horses are well suited for children. Even a six-year-old boy or girl can learn to wash and groom a miniature horse. Older people, people with disabilities, or anyone with a love for horses but frightened of their big size can enjoy these animals.

### The Smallest Horse

Horses of any size are measured from the **withers**\* to the ground. The withers is a point on the horse's back near the end of its mane. Miniature

\*Words in **bold type** are explained in the glossary at the end of this book.

A young girl gets to know a miniature horse. Both are about the same height.

horses measure 34 inches (87 centimeters) or less in height, and some are as small as 25 inches (64 centimeters). Ponies are larger, between 35 and 58 inches (90 and 149 centimeters) high at the withers. Standard horses measure more than 58 inches, which is about twice the size of miniatures. Very large horses such as the Clydesdale or the Shire can be as tall as 6 feet (1.8 meters). This is about three times the height of the smallest miniature horses!

Besides their small size, how are miniature horses different from other horses and ponies? Actually, there isn't much difference, and that is what makes miniatures so special. The goal of miniature horse breeders is to raise horses that look exactly like standard horses.

One difference, though, may be noticeable. The miniature horse is smaller, but its tail and mane are sometimes as long and thick as those of a standard horse. A miniature's tail may even drag on the ground like a bridal train.

A miniature horse stands in front of a full-size horse at Winner's Circle Ranch in Petaluma, California.

To find other differences, a closer look at the miniature horse is necessary. The miniature's hoof—the tough, horny material covering its foot—is very thick. And because the miniature horse weighs much less than a full-size horse, it does not usually need to wear horseshoes to protect its hooves.

13

More than any single feature, however, size sets apart miniatures from other horses. Miniatures weigh between 100 and 300 pounds (45 and 136 kilograms). The largest horses weigh more than 2,000 pounds (909 kilograms). One owner jokingly claims there is only one difference between a miniature and a full-size horse. If a miniature horse steps on your foot, he says, your bones will not be broken.

## *Personality Plus*

A newborn miniature horse, called a **foal**, weighs between 18 and 22 pounds (8 and 10 kilograms) and stands about 16 to 20 inches (41 to 52 centimeters) tall. Some have been reported to stand just 12 inches (31 centimeters) at birth. In fact, these babies are small enough to pick up and cuddle.

Because miniature horses are small, many are treated as pets. They often spend hours each day with their owners, and sometimes take part in the daily activities of their human family. Many people

A curious foal sniffs at a boot.

believe that early handling makes miniatures gentler and easier to train than full-size horses.

Horses are herd animals, and they enjoy being with other animals. Most horses choose another horse for a companion. Because of their size, miniature horses also make friends with dogs, goats, sheep, and even chickens.

Miniatures enjoy human companions as well. Curious and playful, they are sometimes a nuisance when people are busy. One owner, while trying to mend a fence, was bumped repeatedly by his miniature horse. When he turned around, he discovered the mischievous horse had stolen all his tools.

Intelligent animals, miniatures learn quickly. Some have been taught unusual tricks, such as pushing shopping carts and opening drawers for their owners. Others are taught to compete in jumping contests, obstacle courses, or driving events. Only small children can ride miniature horses, because these horses cannot support much weight on their backs. Still, many people find that riding in a cart or wagon behind them is just as much fun. One miniature horse can pull two adults in a cart for ten miles (16 kilometers). A team of miniature horses can pull a wagon with several people in it.

Although most miniatures are friendly around

This miniature horse has made friends with a dog.          17

The team of miniature horses at this wedding pulls one wagon, while a team of full-size horses pulls another, larger one.

people, they have as much spirit as their large relatives. When a strange horse, big or small, enters its territory, a miniature **stallion** will issue a threatening scream. Owners report that full-size stallions have been driven off by miniature horses. One owner watched her miniature stallion bully several full-size horses while guarding its **mare**.

### Visitors Welcome

Where can you find these unusual horses? They live in some surprising places—perhaps in your own neighborhood! Because miniature horses need less space than standard horses, some people keep them as backyard pets. This arrangement can cause problems.

One miniature horse named Ragtime ate alongside the family dog, napped in the living room, and rode in the back seat of the family car. But neighbors wanted Ragtime to move away because horses were not allowed in their neighborhood. Sometimes such an argument must be settled in a court of law.

In Oakland, California, Rayford Ely takes his miniature horses to visit residents of nursing homes and students in schools. Because of their good work, the mayor of Oakland declared Ely's horses a "city treasure" and allowed him to keep his animals in his large backyard.

Miniature horses around the house can create

In many places, miniature horses have become part of the family.
This one watches television with its human owner.

funny situations. Once, Ely thought one of his "treasures" had been stolen. Everyone in the household looked frantically for Playboy, a small brown stallion. They were about to call the police when someone noticed the door to the guest house was open. Inside, gazing contentedly out a window, was Playboy!

Most miniature horses live on farms and ranches, and some of these places allow visitors. Winners' Circle Ranch in Petaluma, California, and the Gettysburg miniature horse farm in Gettysburg, Pennsylvania, are open for tourists in the spring and summer. Here, the visitors and miniatures take a close look at each other. The small horses sniff at people's pockets and poke soft muzzles into their hands. Visitors see the miniatures in pastures and stables, take buckboard wagon rides, and watch the horses perform in shows.

In Texas, Sister Bernadette Mueller began raising miniature horses to provide income for the Monastery of Saint Clare. At first, visitors were

Sister Bernadette Mueller with a miniature horse and other animals at the Monastery of Saint Clare in Brenham, Texas.

always welcome at the monastery. Later, the miniature horses became so popular that the visitors often interrupted the daily prayer schedule. Sister Bernadette was forced to limit visiting to two hours every afternoon.

One hundred years ago, only a small number of miniature horses lived throughout the world.

Today, miniatures are found in nearly every American state and Canadian province. In the United States, Texas has the largest number, followed by California and Florida. These three states have more than half of all registered miniatures.

The little horses now live in many other countries as well—Australia, Great Britain, Belgium, Denmark, Germany, The Netherlands, Argentina, Panama, Venezuela, South Africa, New Zealand, and Japan. Miniatures are especially well suited to Japan, a crowded nation where there is little open space. In all these places around the world, people are raising miniature horses and discovering what makes them so special.

Miniature horses are actually larger than their earliest ancestors. *Eohippus*, the dawn horse, is shown in this drawing.

# Chapter 2

# Mystery of a History

No one knows where miniature horses were first found or bred. One story tells of a canyon where a herd of large horses was trapped. Because food was scarce, the horses produced smaller and smaller babies. Depending on the storyteller, this mysterious canyon is reported to be in different parts of the world. Even if we do not know the true story of the first miniature horses, we do know some of their interesting history.

### The Dawn Horse

The miniature horse is not nearly as small as its earliest ancestors. About 60 million years ago, a creature named **eohippus**, also known as the dawn horse, lived in the subtropical forests of North

America and Europe. Eohippus was only 16 inches (41 centimeters) tall, about the size of a small dog.

When the earth's climate cooled, some of the forests became grassy plains. The descendants of the dawn horse changed in several ways. One change, or **adaptation**, was increased size and strength. In the forest, it was easy for eohippus to hide. On the flat plains, the horses needed longer legs to speed away from **predators**. These new horses developed tough hooves to help them run on the hard ground. Their necks lengthened so they could reach the low-growing grasses, and their teeth adapted for grinding. With their increased size, they had larger brains, which helped them survive in a more difficult environment.

It took about 50 million years for modern horses to develop from the dawn horse. Still, these modern horses were not as large as today's standard horses. They were the size of today's ponies. Horses probably would have remained small if they had not been tamed and used to help fight wars.

Over millions of years, the necks of horses lengthened so they could reach the low-growing grasses of the plains.

Horses were first **domesticated** about 4,000 years ago in Asia. People began to use them in wars, at first to haul supplies, and later to carry soldiers. Because of war, the domesticated horse spread throughout the world. Much later, when soldiers began to wear heavy armor, the horses needed to be bigger and stronger. To raise larger and larger horses, people bred the biggest stallions and mares. The largest of today's horses are descended from these war horses.

In England, war nearly brought an end to all small horses. King Henry VIII lost so many horses in his wars that he worried there would not be enough large horses to replace them. He ordered that all horses less than 56 inches (142 centimeters) in height be destroyed. Fortunately for ponies and miniature horses, his orders were not carried out.

Just as horses were bred larger for war and heavy work, they could be made smaller by breeding the smallest stallions and mares. Some owners believe that the first miniature horses appeared in the 1500s and were the pets of kings and queens in Europe. Unfortunately, very little is known about these royal horses.

In the 1700s, small horses performed in traveling circuses. At Astley's circus in England, a small horse about three feet tall became popular for its mind-reading tricks. In another well-known circus act, a pair of small horses dressed in hats sat down to take tea with the clown. Often, monkeys rode on the small horses to the delight of everyone in the circus audience.

### *Working in the Coal Mines*

Small horses were not just entertainers—Shetland and Welsh ponies from the British Isles pulled tubs of coal in coal mines. These "pit ponies" went to work underground at the age of four years. Often, they spent their entire working lives below ground, but they were well cared for in their underground stables. Miners enjoyed the companionship of the pit ponies. Stories tell of miners risking their lives to save the horses during mine cave-ins.

Before 1914, there were 70,000 working horses in coal mines. They began to compete in above ground contests at county shows and became quite popular with the general public. As pit ponies retired, many people asked to adopt them.

### *Coming to America*

Some of these small horses were brought to North America to work in the coal mines of the eastern United States. Eventually, most of them were replaced with machines. Although machinery can move coal faster than the pit ponies, miners say they miss sharing lunch with the horses.

In the early 1900s, Norman Fields of Bedford, Virginia, began to buy pit ponies from Europe for use in the Appalachian coal mines. Sometimes he noticed very small horses among the ones that arrived in America. Fields kept these smallest horses and used them to raise his own herd. By 1964 he had 50 miniature horses in his herd, but most of them never left the area near his Virginia home.

The person who did the most to develop the modern miniature horse breed was Smith McCoy of Rodderfield, West Virginia. He began to buy and sell ponies as a hobby, and found that the smallest horses brought the highest prices. By 1956, he had

A British coal miner and a pit pony share the hardships of working underground.

decided to raise only "midget ponies," his name for miniature horses.

McCoy started his herd by buying the smallest horses he could find anywhere in the United States—all were less than 32 inches (82 centimeters) tall. Then he bred the smallest stallions and mares until he had the world's largest herd of miniature horses. In 1967 Smith McCoy sold his herd of miniatures to breeders from all over America.

Since that time, miniature horses have become popular across the United States and around the world. During the 1970s, several registries were formed to recognize the miniature horse as a separate breed. Such registries list animals that meet the standards for a particular breed.

The American Miniature Horse Association (AMHA), started in Texas in 1978, maintains a well-known registry for miniature horses. Until 1987, the AMHA accepted all miniature horses that met its standards. Then the registry was

Miniature horses must meet the standards set by the American Miniature Horse Association and the American Miniature Horse Registry.

closed to encourage owners to breed only registered animals. Now the AMHA will accept only
the foals born to registered mares.

Another group, the American Miniature Horse
Registry in Peoria, Illinois, has registered American
miniature horses since 1972. To be accepted by this
open registry, miniatures must meet certain standards for size and physical features.

Outside the United States, the Falabella family
of Argentina in South America began to raise miniature horses in 1868. On the Falabella farm near
Buenos Aires, Argentina's capital, the family developed its herd by breeding small horses with other
small horses. The Falabellas used the horses in
their herd as pets and to pull small wagons.

For a long time, the Falabellas did not allow
any of their breeding animals to leave Argentina.
During the 1980s, the family did sell a few
breeding animals in the United States. Today,
Falabella horses attract visitors to the Gettysburg
miniature horse farm in Pennsylvania.

Today's miniature horses are the result of many years of careful breeding and hard work by people in America and around the world. As miniature horses have become more popular, the number of miniature horse farms and ranches has increased rapidly. These are the places where these remarkable animals are born and bred.

# Chapter 3

# Life on a Miniature Horse Ranch

Many things are smaller on a miniature horse ranch than on a ranch for larger horses. Smaller stalls mean more miniature horses can be sheltered in the barn. Exercise rings and corrals are much smaller, too. One acre (.4 hectare) is not enough pasture land for even a single full-size horse. Yet it is enough for three miniature horses.

There are just as many chores, however, on a miniature horse ranch. Small horses have all the same needs as large horses.

### Eating Like a Horse

Early in the morning, miniature horses are fed alfalfa hay and grain. Then they are taken to the

Many farms and ranches in the United States, Canada, and other countries raise miniature horses.

Stalls for miniature horses are smaller than those for full-size horses.

pastures for exercise and grazing. While the horses play and chase each other, the people who run the ranch work hard cleaning out stalls. Bacteria can breed in dirty stalls and spread sickness among the horses. Before they eat too much in the pasture, the horses are returned to their clean stalls.

Miniature horses usually have hay and two

meals of grain each day. They eat one-tenth as much food as full-size horses. As a result, the food bill on a miniature horse ranch is much smaller than on a ranch with large horses.

Diets must be watched very carefully, because horses of all sizes have delicate digestive systems. If they eat too much or eat too fast without chewing properly, the food may become stuck in the intestines, where it can cause pain and even death. This serious condition, called **colic**, is the number one killer of horses both big and small.

## *Grooming*

While the horses are out in the corrals or pasture, they enjoy stretching and rolling in the sunshine. Burrs stick to their thick fur and to their manes and tails. They must be brushed regularly to prevent the burrs from harming the miniatures' skin.

Horse fur grows thicker and longer in the winter, and miniature horses grow especially long winter coats. One of the spring chores on the

For this miniature horse, it's time for a bath.

ranch is to clip the winter coat away. Clipping is followed by a bath with a germ-killing soap and then a good brushing. The miniature horse looks sleek and slender in its summer coat.

Grooming doesn't stop with the miniature horse's fur. Horses walk on the tip of a single "toe" or "finger" in each foot. Over millions of years, the other bones in the horses' feet disappeared. The **hock**, or pointed joint, on the hind leg is like an ankle, and the "knee" on the fore leg is like a wrist. The hoof is like a very thick fingernail around the remaining "toe" or "finger." It never stops growing and must be trimmed about every two months.

A horse's teeth are always growing, too. Long, sharp teeth can cause pain and prevent the horse from chewing its food well. A veterinarian may be needed to rasp, or file, the horse's teeth.

### *Training*

Besides feeding and caring for the health of their miniatures, owners give the horses lessons. Every horse is trained to accept a halter and lead rope, so it can be handled, groomed, and treated by the veterinarian. Miniatures that will perform in horse shows need much more training.

Several steps in training are required when a miniature learns to be a driving horse. First the horse must learn to wear all the pieces of the

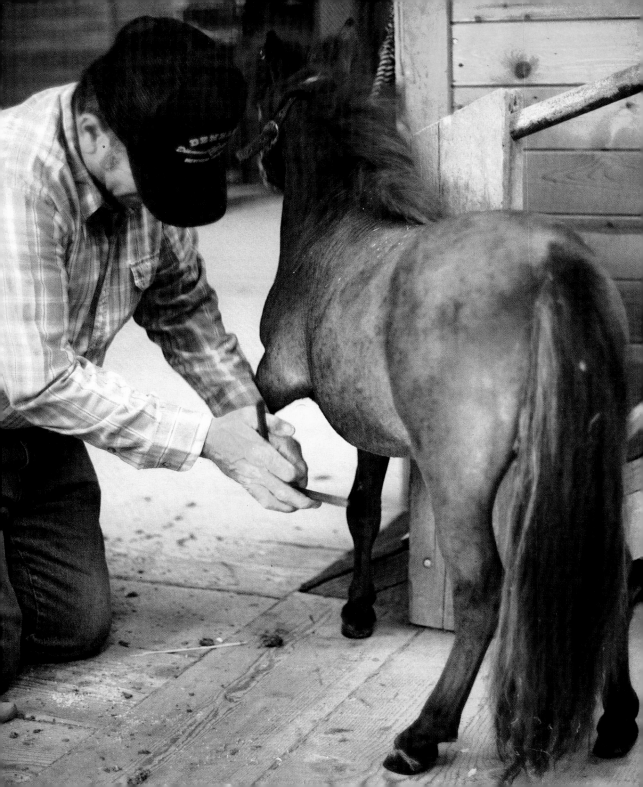

driving harness. A **bridle** with **blinkers** fits over the horse's head, and a **bit** rests in the horse's mouth. **Reins** to control the horse are attached to the bridle. Leather straps wrap around the horse's belly and chest. Several lessons may be needed before the horse is comfortable in a harness.

Next, the trainer walks behind the miniature, guiding it with the reins. After the horse learns to follow the commands of the trainer, a cart is attached to the leather straps around its belly and chest. At this point the trainer still walks instead of riding. Finally, when the horse is comfortable with the weight of the cart, the trainer climbs in and takes a drive. Lessons must be given often and on a regular schedule, or the horse will forget what is expected of it.

## *Foaling*

Late in the day, the miniature horses are fed again and sheltered for the night. Not all of the horses spend the night in the barn. Some stay in

The hoof of a miniature horse must be trimmed because it never stops growing.

A trainer walks behind a miniature horse, guiding it with the reins. Soon the small horse will learn to pull a cart.

the corrals, which have shelters available for cold or wet weather. But night does not always mean a good sleep for the people who live on the ranch. If a pregnant mare is near to giving birth, its owners must be ready to help at any time.

The business of a miniature horse ranch is to raise more miniature horses. Mares are old enough to become mothers when they are 3 years old. They often live 30 years or more and continue having foals throughout their lives.

The miniature mare is pregnant for 11-1/2 months, about the same length of time as a full-size mare. Usually foals are born in early spring or summer and most often at night. Miniature horses sometimes have trouble giving birth. If the foal is too large or is turned the wrong way, a veterinarian will need to be called. Owners keep a close watch on their mares at this time.

Winners' Circle Ranch has a special set of stalls for pregnant mares and mares with newborn foals. A closed-circuit camera keeps an eye on these horses, and the owners can watch them on a video monitor in their house.

Restlessness signals that the mare is in labor. She lies down and gets up frequently. She may turn her head to look at her side. During this time the owners do not disturb the mare. If the horse is nervous, she can slow down the delivery, which can be dangerous for the foal and herself.

When the foal is about to be born, the mare lies down flat on her side with her head resting on the straw. Because the owners have attached a breeder alert system to her halter, an alarm goes off as soon as her head touches the ground. Day or night, when the owners hear the beeper alarm, they rush to the barn.

The foal is born inside a skinlike casing. This casing, the **amniotic sac**, has the same strength and toughness as that of a much larger horse. Sometimes a miniature foal does not have enough strength to break out of the sac. If necessary, the owner breaks through the sac, allowing the newborn horse to breathe. As soon as the foal is safe, the owner backs away to let the mother and baby get acquainted.

The mare licks and nuzzles the foal. Within fifteen or twenty minutes, the baby horse is standing. With a little help from its mother, it finds her udder and begins to nurse.

In a special stall at Winner's Circle Ranch, a newborn foal struggles to its feet under the watchful gaze of its mother.

Watching the birth of a foal is an exciting experience. Now there is a new member in the world of miniature horses. Whether it is a **filly** or a **colt**, its owners hope that this little horse will carry the best traits of the miniature breed to pass on to future generations.

# Chapter 4

# Showing Off

Cats catch mice, and dogs provide guard service. But if you can't ride a miniature horse, what good is it? People often ask this question. Many owners believe these animals make excellent pets and companions for children and for adults. To them, miniature horses are worth having because they are special, not because they are useful.

## Miniatures on Parade

Miniature horses can, however, perform in some remarkable ways. They participate in parades such as the Philadelphia Thanksgiving Day Parade, the Tournament of Roses Parade, and even the presidential Inaugural Parade. In January 1989, sixteen horses from Ashly Acres Miniature Horse Ranch

On January 20, 1989, sixteen horses from Ashly Acres Miniature Horse Ranch in Maryland marched in the Inaugural Parade in Washington, D.C.

in Maryland came to Washington, D.C., to honor
newly elected President George Bush. After a long
delay on a cold, windy afternoon, the miniature
horses started along the parade route past crowds
of cheering people. President Bush saluted and
Barbara Bush waved as the miniatures passed the
reviewing stand.

Miniature horses serve their communities in
other ways. Several ranches welcome visits from
school groups. Often, these students come from
large cities and have never seen horses at close
range. At Christmastime, horses from Ashly Acres
pull a miniature hay wagon complete with a Santa
Claus into the auditorium of a nursing home. Some
little horses visit hospitals, where they cheer up
seriously ill patients. Others are used in the treat-
ment of children and adults who suffer from men-
tal illness. One owner hopes to teach disabled
adults and children how to drive miniature horses.
Perhaps driving miniature horses will someday become a new event in the Special Olympics.

Miniature horses bring joy to people of all ages. This horse enjoys going for a ride.

### *The Show Circuit*

During the summer months, many miniature horse owners travel the show circuit with their animals. At shows the owners hope to win awards that will increase the value of their horses. But these shows are not all competition. The people who take part in them meet old and new friends from around the country. They talk about their horses, sharing experiences of raising and caring for miniatures.

There are many ways for miniature horses and their owners to earn prizes at the shows. In halter class events, the horses are led into the judging ring on a lead rope. Horses are judged in classes with other horses of similar size, age, or sex. The judges look at the horse's features, or **conformation**, as well as how it poses. Using hand gestures and sounds, the person showing the horse tries to keep the miniature standing still and alert with its head raised and ears forward. Children as young as five years old participate.

Children as young as five years old participate in miniature horse shows.

Jumping and driving events are exciting to watch. In **roadster** events, a single miniature horse is hitched to a racing cart. The driver wears colorful racing silks and shows his or her ability to control the horse at three different speeds, or **gaits**. The driver must be able to change the horse's gait at the judge's request. In "pleasure driving" events,

A miniature horse pulls a driver dressed in an old-fashioned costume in a "pleasure driving" event.

drivers dress in fancy, old-fashioned costumes, and they are a pleasure to watch.

Both roadster and pleasure driving have events for young people less than eighteen years of age. But driving horses is not easy. It requires training, knowledge, and experience for the driver as well as the horse.

Many young people enjoy taking part in the jumping events. In the "hunter" class events, the horse goes over a series of jumps while its master runs alongside. In "jumper" events, the master is allowed to jump with the horse. Miniatures usually make the jumps successfully, but some people have been embarrassed when they tripped and fell.

### Miniatures in the Future

Today, there are at least 12,000 miniature horses, and their number is growing rapidly. In the future this lively little breed of horses may begin to replace its full-size relatives in cities and suburbs where people have less space to raise large animals. The miniatures' easy care and gentle nature make them popular pets. More and more of them will appear in parades, newspapers, magazines, and on television. Miniature horses are here to stay, and one may come to your neighborhood soon.

# Sources of Information about Miniature Horses

If you would like to find out more about miniature horses or learn where you can see miniature horses and shows in your area, write to:

The American Miniature Horse Association
2908 S.E. Loop 820
Fort Worth, Texas 76140

American Miniature Horse Registry
P.O. Box 3415
Peoria, Illinois 61614

The following ranches invite tourists to spend a day visiting miniature horses and watching them perform. For details, write to:

Flying M Ranch
3400 N.W. 60th St.
Ocala, Florida 32675

Gettysburg Land of Little Horses
P.O. Box 36
Gettysburg, Pennsylvania 17325

Monastery Miniature Horse Ranch
Monastery of St. Clare
Rt. 7 Box 7504 Highway 105
Brenham, Texas 77833

Winners' Circle Ranch
5911 Lakeville Highway
Petaluma, California 94952

# Glossary

**adaptation (ad-ap-TAY-shuhn)**—the way that animals or plants adjust to their surroundings to increase their chances for survival

**amniotic sac (am-nee-AHT-ihk sak)**—in horses, the sac in which the baby develops inside the mother

**bit**—a piece of metal which fits inside a horse's mouth and is attached to the bridle; the bit is used to control the horse

**blinkers**—square pieces attached to the bridle which keep the horse from seeing to its right or left side; also called blinders or winkers

**bridle**—leather straps which fit over the horse's head and to which the bit and reins are attached

**colic (CAH-lihk)**—indigestion or pain in the stomach or intestines; especially dangerous for horses

**colt**—a young male horse

**conformation (cahn-fohr-MAY-shuhn)**—the proportions and features of the horse

**domesticated (doh-MEHS-tuh-kay-tuhd)**—used here to describe animals that have been tamed for use by humans

**eohippus (ee-oh-HIHP-uhs)**—an early ancestor of the modern horse that lived about 60 million years ago in the subtropical forests of North America and Europe; also known as the dawn horse

**filly**—a young female horse

**foal**—a baby horse

**gaits (gayts)**—ways of moving forward such as the walk, trot, canter, and gallop

**hock (hahk)**—the pointed, backward-bending joint on the hind leg of a horse and other animals; on a human, the ankle is the same joint as the hock

**mare**—a female horse

**muzzle (MUHZ-uhl)**—the mouth, nose, and jaws of an animal

**predators (PREHD-uh-tuhrz)**—animals which hunt other animals for food

**reins (raynz)**—long straps of leather attached to a horse's bridle; used to guide and control the horse

**roadster (ROHD-stuhr)**—a light, open racing cart with two wheels and a seat

**stallion**—a male horse

**withers**—the highest point on the back of a horse, located between the shoulder blades, near the last hairs of the mane

# Index

American Miniature Horse Association (AMHA), 32
American Miniature Horse Registry, 34
amniotic sac, 46
appearance, 9, 12, 37
Ashly Acres Miniature Horse Ranch, 49-50
breeding, 28, 31, 32, 34
circuses, 28-29
coal mines, 29, 31
colic, 39
colt, 47
conformation, 52
Ely, Rayford, 19, 21
eohippus, 25-26
equipment, 43
exercise, 38
Falabella family, the, 34
Fields, Norman, 31
filly, 47
foaling, 44-46
foals, 14, 34
food, 37, 38-39, 43
gait, 53
Gettysburg miniature horse farm, 21, 34
Henry VIII, 28
herds, 15
hooves, 13, 40-41
horses, standard: domestication of, 27; evolution of, 26; size of, 12; uses for, 27
horse shows: driving events in, 52; jumping events in, 53, 55; ranches and, 21; training for, 41, 43
intelligence, 17
life span, 45
location, 23, 24
McCoy, Smith, 31, 32
manes, 12
mare, 18, 34, 35
Monastery of Saint Clare, 21-22
origin, 22, 25, 28
parades, 49, 50
pets, 14, 19, 21, 28, 34, 49
ponies, 29, 32
popularity, 32, 35
population, 22, 23, 55
ranches, 21, 35, 37, 44, 50
size, 12
sounds, 18
stallion, 18
tails, 12
teeth, 41
training, 41, 43
tricks, 17
uses, 49, 50
weight, 13, 14
Winners' Circle Ranch, 21, 45
withers, 10

59

## About the Author

As an elementary school teacher in Berkeley, California, Gail LaBonte has shared her love and knowledge of animals with many students. She has studied wildlife firsthand in Africa while assisting her husband in zoological field research. Close to home in San Francisco, she enjoys observing animals while backpacking or tidepooling along the Pacific Coast with her husband and two children, Jason and Alison. The author is a member of the Society of Children's Book Writers. She is also the author of *The Llama* and *The Arctic Fox*, two other Remarkable Animals books.